Hidden in Plain Sight

Hidden in Plain Sight

History and Architecture of the
Airton Meeting House

by

Laurel Phillipson

and

Alison Armstrong

with an introduction by

Chris Skidmore

Quacks Books
Q

First Published 2017
© Copyright Laurel Phillipson, Alison Armstrong & Chris Skidmore 2017

Published by Quacks Books, Petergate, York

British library cataloguing in publication data
Laurel Phillipson, Alison Armstrong, 2017
Hidden in Plain Sight

isbn 978-1-904446-77-4

Set in **Baskerville** twelve point roman, justified with occasional emboldening and italicising with one and a half point inter line leading, headings centered in eighteen point Baskerville bold, running heads verso ten point bold, recto twelve point italic, gutter margin seventeen millimetres, head margin twenty millimetres, fore-edge margin twenty two millimetres and foot margin twenty five millimetres. Illustrated with photographs, drawings and maps.

Printed by offset lithography on 100gsm paper, chosen for its sustainability, folded, section sewn and bound with a laminated card cover by Quacks the Printer, 7 Grape lane, Petergate York Yo1 7hu, t 0044 (0)1904 635967, info@quacks.info, www.radiusonline.info

Contents

Preface

In studying the Airton Meeting House, the principal authors have each taken very different approaches and have worked amicably but independently of one another. While Laurel has worked almost entirely with the historian's tools of manuscripts, printed ephemera and published books, Alison has consulted the buildings themselves, looking at their plans and at the materials, methods and details of their construction. The result of these disparate approaches has been to produce a book of two distinct parts: a narrative history for the first half and a vernacular buildings survey report for the second. We have not attempted to fuse these into a single text in the expectation that you, our readers, may find it interesting to see what information is produced by these very different approaches to the study of the same set of buildings. It has been gratifying to us to discover that the diverse types of evidence which we have consulted agree with and support one another, enabling us to reveal an unexpected narrative of the unusual origins, history and antiquity of the Airton Meeting House and its associated buildings.

Dedication

This book is dedicated with gratitude to all who have worshipped in and cared for the Airton Meeting House in the past and to all who will do so in the future.

Fig. 2

Acknowledgements

Among the many people we would like to thank for their encouragement and assistance in preparing this book are the members of our respective families and the members of Airton Friends Meeting. We gratefully acknowledge financial and material assistance provided by Sessions Book Trust and by the Quakers in Yorkshire Outreach Fund. We thank Michael Sessions, Horst Meyer and the staff at Quacks Printers and Publishers for their assistance and advice. We also record with grateful remembrance the contributions of three who are no longer with us: Kevin Berry, Brian Foxley and Richard Harland, each of whom contributed greatly to the restoration of the Airton Meeting House. Without their active involvement nothing might have been achieved and this book never written.

Introduction

The growth of Nonconformity

The growth of discontent with the religious order supported by the State (established religion) in England has a long history. It went along with two other changes – the increasing availability of the Bible for private reading and the growth of those classes in society that had the leisure to give to reading and considering it. Comparison with the state of the church in the first century as described in the New Testament led to dissatisfaction with the church as it had become. The simplicity of Jesus of Nazareth's teachings compared to the complexity of medieval theology led many to strive for personal salvation by following his example. Along with this often went an assurance that personal religious experience could form a firm foundation for a good life and that a dependence on priests and sacraments was not necessary. These movements pre-date the Reformation of the mid-sixteenth century and continued well after it. In England they began in the late-fourteenth century with the followers of John Wyclif, known as Lollards. Here in the Yorkshire-Lancashire borders there was a movement (Grindletonianism) in the early-sixteenth century based on the teaching of Roger Brearley, who was curate at Grindleton, near Clitheroe, and at Kildwick in Craven. Teaching might come, as in these cases, from clergy with dissenting views or from itinerant preachers following a similar calling to the medieval friars. Often the laity were important in the organisation of these groups; like-minded folk would meet in each other's houses to read the scriptures and pray together. They might know of others with similar views in neighbouring towns or villages without there being any formal association. They might continue to worship on Sundays in the local parish church rather than running the risk of the legal penalties that the ecclesiastical courts could exact for non-attendance or heresy.

Because these groups operated outside the established church we often have little information about their importance or their numbers. However, the profound social changes that were brought about in the mid-seventeenth century by the Civil Wars and the ensuing Commonwealth, which included freedom from censorship, resulted in a vast increase in the written record of the variety of religious views espoused in England. Those who felt they were called to preach their truth did so, not completely without restraint. We also know that many dissenting views were encouraged by the chaplains of the various regiments of the New Model Army. There were still those, however, who kept their own counsel and worshipped in the parish church, where the clergy might themselves preach a variety of gospels. Increasingly those unhappy with what the parish church provided began to form, particularly in the towns and cities, separated churches with formal covenants, membership and clerical leadership.

Among the groups which arose to prominence in this period, and which are important to the Airton story are the Seekers and the Quakers. Seekers, as their name implies, had often not only been disappointed by the established church but had been involved in one or other of the separated churches too. The essence of the Seeker position was *a belief that the powers and authority granted to the apostles in the New Testament had been so corrupted and destroyed by the Church of Rome that no true church could be constituted until God had raised up a new race of apostles* [Watts 1978: p.185]. Seekers met for worship together in expectant waiting for the arrival of an apostle. Folk became increasingly drawn to this position in the 1640s and 1650s and Seeker groups sprang up in a number of places. Although there were local concentrations of Seeker groups, such as those in Swaledale and Westmorland, it is not known to what extent they had any regional organisation similar to the associations set up by the Baptists in the 1650s.

The beginnings of Quakerism

George Fox (1624-1691) grew up in a Puritan family in Leicestershire and left home at 19 to seek 'the truth' for himself. Through the turbulent years of the Civil Wars he wandered the Midlands seeking out people and groups who might help him in his search, but also occasionally preaching and demonstrating against what he saw as the corruption of the world, suffering imprisonment from time to time. He came to believe that everyone was able to have direct access to God, who, in the person of Christ, would act as their 'Inward Teacher', thus bypassing the need for churches and their clergy. This was the message that he brought when he travelled north in May 1652. What we know of this journey and the other events of Fox's early life derives from accounts which he dictated first in 1664 and then more fully in 1675-8 and which were constructed into a narrative by other hands and published in 1694, three years after his death, as *A Journal or Historical Account of the Life … of … George Fox*. From the few places identified, it is generally thought that Fox travelled from Pendle Hill on the borders of Lancashire *via* Wensleydale to Sedbergh. As Laurel Phillipson points out, this journey is likely to have taken him through Malhamdale.

Eventually, after preaching at a hiring-fair in Sedbergh, Fox came into contact with a group of Seekers who met in an isolated chapel on Firbank Fell in Westmorland (now Cumbria). When he preached to them, they recognised in him the apostle that they were waiting for, and this pattern was repeated in a number of neighbouring Seeker groups. A young man present at one of these meetings recalled that, *George Fox stood up in the mighty power of God, and in the demonstration thereof was his mouth opened to preach Christ Jesus, the light of life and the way to God, and saviour of all that believe and obey him, which was delivered in that power and authority that most of the auditory, which were several hundreds, were effectually reached to the heart, and convinced of the Truth that very day, for it was the day of God's power. A notable day indeed never to be forgotten by me, Thomas Camm, … I being then present at that meeting, a school boy but about 12 years of age.* The meeting of Fox and the Westmorland Seekers led to the movement which eventually became the Religious Society of Friends. From these groups people were inspired to go out and preach the Quaker message across the whole country and abroad. Their success was such that by 1680 it is thought that there were as many as 60,000 Quakers in England and Wales (1.15% of the population).

Quakers in Airton

How Quakerism came to Malhamdale has always been somewhat of a mystery. The reports of early Quaker beginnings, collected nationally in the early 1700s, make no mention of this dale, despite quite detailed reports from Quaker groups in Wharfedale and around Skipton and Settle. That there were earlier groups in the area is supported by the evidence of Friends in Settle: *Before the Testimony of Truth, or the way of worshipping God in spirit, was published or declared in this latter age, by the messengers & servants of the Lord in these parts of the Country [county], there was much talk & discoursing of a people that were scattered up and down the Country, and more especially in the west and north parts thereof, that differed from other people in their belief concerning the principles of religion and worshipping of God…* [Penny 1907: p.302].

It is clear, too, that the Meeting House which William and Alice Ellis secured for the Quakers of Malhamdale in 1700 is a substantial structure, more impressive than others built nearby, such as those at Farfield and Skipton. It was capable of seating a considerable number of Friends. Only that at Settle is on a comparable scale. How and why it came to be built at Airton raises a number of further questions. Therefore it is good at last to have an account of the history and architecture of Airton Meeting House which attempts not only to document the building and its past but to begin to offer answers to these mysteries.

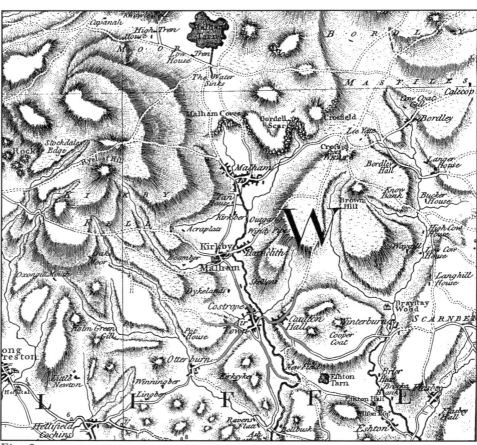

Fig. 3

History

1600 - 1651

Airton in the early seventeenth century was a small obscure village in the heart of the Yorkshire Dales, about nine miles north-west of Skipton, consisting of little more than a few houses and a water-powered corn mill, situated by a minor river crossing on an ancient route that runs in an almost straight line between upper Wharfedale and Clitheroe. The village's one unusual feature was the number of roads and lanes leading into it from all directions. Six of these are now paved roads, including two alternative ways to Skipton, one through Eshton and Gargrave and another through Winterburn and Rylstone.

The seventh is a former drove road from Clitheroe into Upper Wharfedale by way of Hellifield, Otterburn, Airton, Bordley and along Mastiles Lane to Kilnsey. This was probably the route from Pendle Hill taken by George Fox and Richard Farnsworth in June 1652, when Fox travelled to the Seekers' annual gathering and midsummer fair at Sedbergh. It was more used in those days than it is today. This route's northern portion, from Hellifield to Kilnsey, is now within the Yorkshire Dales National Park; it remains a very pleasant walk on a sunny day. The combination of local obscurity and numerous access routes made Airton a good place for people to assemble without being much observed. So long as they travelled by diverse routes little notice would be taken of their comings and goings, and once they were congregated in Airton there would be few people about to notice their gathering.

Two fields on the east side of Airton, between the crossroads and the water-powered corn-mill, were at the heart of the estate that was the home of Major General John Lambert, who led the New Model Army in Scotland. During much of the Civil War, he was second in command to Oliver Cromwell; he also drafted the Articles of Government of the Protectorate, for which he is insufficiently honoured as a pioneer of constitutional democracy. The Lambert family's dower house stood in the more northerly of these two fields. Less than 200 yards away in the neighbouring field was the building that is now Airton Quaker Meeting House. It was almost in sight of the Lambert seat, or family house, that stood on the hill just a mile away in Calton.

Fig. 4

The Airton corn mill was replaced first by a water- and then by a steam-powered spinning mill. During the Second World War, the village's obscurity was taken advantage of when the mill buildings were used to house a secret plant for the manufacture of an essential supply: Dettol for cleaning operating theatres and the injuries of war-wounded soldiers. However, an accidental spill soon divulged the secret. The River Aire is said to have reeked of Dettol all the way down to Skipton. More recently, the mill buildings have been converted to small flats.

Airton Meeting House is a barn-like structure that was built early in the seventeenth century, or possibly late in the sixteenth, on the foundations of an older, thatch-roofed cruck barn whose remaining traces include the foundation stones most clearly visible at the east end of the present-day building, plus some repositioned cruck timbers that were reused to form an early seventeenth century open truss in the loft of the present meeting house, and the present building's layout which repeats that of its older predecessor.

Fig. 5

The earlier building's foundations were retained when it was rebuilt as, or replaced by, the present Meeting House. The first building was a stone-built, four-bay barn. At its western end was a small structure, perhaps a room with an open fireplace, that was the precursor of the present cottage (The Nook). External entrance to the demolished cruck barn would almost certainly have been in its northern side, facing the road. A possible threshold of a secondary entrance remains visible in the footings of its eastern gable end. The present Meeting House repeats the ground plan of the barn it replaced. The Nook is now a private residence and is not generally open to visitors.

The Meeting House we have today faces away from the road. Entrance to its large room was in the early seventeenth century, as it is now, in the centre of its southern wall. When it was built on the foundations of the older structure, part of the hillslope on its east and south sides was cut away to allow access from the south. At the same time, the threshold of the Meeting House's south-facing doorway was cut below the top of the retained foundations of the former barn. The demolished barn would have had low walls and a steep, cruck-framed, ling-thatched roof, similar to but larger than a heavily restored barn at Grimwith High Laithe. Its replacement had a stone roof very like what it has now.

Extensive building repairs carried out in 2010 uncovered the original external doorway of The Nook, in its south wall (to the right of a more recent doorway between the cottage and The Barn) with a window alongside. Separating the large meeting room from the cottage is a stout cross-wall with an open fireplace and an alcove alongside, which may mark the position of a former narrow communicating door between the dwelling and the meeting room. Built into the stone chimney breast of the fireplace is an oak beam that may originally have supported a wattle and clay fire-hood. While this could perhaps be a remnant of the pre-seventeenth-century structure, it is more likely to be an example of rural conservatism in fireplace construction.

We do not know exactly when the Meeting House was erected. If it was built by or for Major General Lambert, this could have been in the 1640s, but that is unlikely as he was mostly away from home and heavily engaged militarily and politically during that and the following two decades. If, as is more probable, it was built by his father or grandfather, it would have been between about 1600 and 1620. Architecturally, an earlier date is most likely. The late Brian Foxley, RIBA, identified the open truss structure of the loft of the Meeting House as being of early seventeenth century construction incorporating re-used elements of the earlier cruck roof. A few features perhaps hint at a late sixteenth century date, but may in fact be evidence of rural conservatism. Whatever the exact age of the Meeting House, it could only have been built and used with the Lambert family's full knowledge and approval.

Fig. 6

The Major General's father, who was also named John Lambert, died in 1632, by which time most of the Lambert estate was mortgaged or in the hands of trustees. At the time of his father's death, the future Major General was aged 13. He married Frances Lister in 1639 and soon became fully involved in serving the Parliamentary cause. He replaced Lord Fairfax as leader of the New Model Army, was appointed Governor of Oxford in 1646 and Major General of the Five Northern Counties in 1647. In 1650, Oliver Cromwell was appointed Commander in Chief, with Major General Lambert as Second in Command. Lambert was sent to Edinburgh in 1651 to make a final settlement with Scotland. In February 1652, he was appointed Lord Deputy of Ireland and in May of the same year he bought a large house in Wimbledon, in keeping with his elevated status. However, also in May of the same year and before the new house was ready for occupation, the appointment was rescinded and given instead to General Fleetwood, who was affianced to Oliver Cromwell's recently widowed daughter, Bridget Ireton. It was reported that Frances Lambert and Bridget Ireton quarrelled over this appointment in public, in St. James's Park. At this point, it is most probable that John and Frances

Lambert would have returned to their Yorkshire home, to consider what to do next and to avoid being in London at the time of Bridget's wedding. It is known that they were living in Calton later in 1652.

The above sequence of events, plus the fact that by 1630 the Lambert family finances were in poor shape and most of the family estate was mortgaged, strongly suggest that the Airton Meeting House was built early in the seventeenth century. It also equally strongly suggests that Major General John Lambert and his wife would have been at home in Calton in late May and early June 1652, at the very time when George Fox and Richard Farnsworth were travelling northwards from Pendle Hill.

Fig. 7

Several features of the early seventeenth century building make it clear that despite its superficial appearance it was never intended to be used as a barn. Most notably, until the last decade of that century it had no windows or doors facing north onto the street, no way carts could be brought close to off-load fodder, food or fleeces, and no entrance for livestock. Nor were there wind-holes to provide a through draught for winnowing grain. Another telling feature is that the space that would have housed animals in the earlier building did not in its seventeenth century replacement have a stone- or cobble-paved floor. Inspection while the building was being restored in 2008 showed that it had always been wood-floored. Furthermore, cattle barns almost always have their barnyards at the same level or below that of the barn doors in order to prevent winter rain and muck flooding in. With its only external door in the middle of its south, uphill, wall there was no place for a barnyard.

Fig. 8

In order to permit entrance from the south side of the building, ground was cut away on its eastern gable end and along the southern face, exposing the plinth-like tops of the substantial footings of the earlier structure and forming a sunken corridor eight feet wide backed by a four-foot high retaining wall or revetment with an integral stone bench. Clearly, these features were designed for people, not for animals. Their unobtrusive but deliberately intended effect was to shield the entrance to the building and the activities of its users from oversight by casual passers-by. A stone-arched gateway across the path to the Meeting House is contemporary with the early seventeenth century building. Probably it had originally had a full-height wooden door, which would have added to the privacy of the building's users. Adjacent to the east end of the building was a small walled burial ground.

Fig. 9

Although its appearance was and is barn-like, the building was conceived and built as a meeting house capable of accommodating more than 100 people. It was deliberately made inconspicuous by its semi-concealed entrance, by its absence of doors or windows facing onto the road, and by its absence of decorative features. Referring to a preaching visit he made in the mid to late 1650s, Gervase Benson, who was first a Seeker and later a Quaker leader, described this Meeting House as *a barn in a field in Airton*. It was intended to look like a barn, but was in fact purpose-built as a meeting house and was used as such for at least some decades, perhaps for more than half a century, before the advent of Quakerism in our area. For whose meetings was it originally intended?

There was, particularly in the north of England in the sixteenth and early seventeenth centuries, an attractive but elusive religious group known as the Seekers. These people favoured a large measure of religious toleration and refused to join any of the more prominent religious factions that arose during those centuries. At a time when people were killing one another over disputes about systems of church government and questions of whether there should be an altar at the east end of a church or a communion table in the centre of its nave, who can blame them? Because most of the religious controversies they encountered were over matters of ritual, dogma, creeds, priests, and sermons, the Seekers rejected all of these observances, which they judged to be corrupted or inessential elements of religion. Instead, they met without ordained clergy, to wait in silence until God would show them a better way of worshipping. The Seekers introduced practices which Quakers also adopted, of unordained laity praying and worshipping in silence. Another characteristic of the Seekers was that they avoided persecution by being deliberately unobtrusive. Most Seeker individuals did not openly identify themselves as such. Neither did they keep lists of members, proselytize, or engage in religious debates or controversies. When, for example, they wanted to hold a major gathering in 1652, they scheduled this to coincide with the annual hiring fair at Sedbergh. That way, people travelling to the Seeker meeting , if asked where they were going, could say that they were going to the fair, and once arrived at the fair it would be difficult to distinguish between those who had come to attend the Seeker meeting and those who had come to hire maidservants or farmhands.

Fig. 10

A building almost indistinguishable from a barn, in a small rural village accessible by a variety of routes is just what might be expected as a Seeker meeting place. Our Meeting House's relatively large size implies a large catchment area and something more than local significance. At this time, Skipton was at least a regional headquarters of the Seeker movement. Thomas Taylor, who with his brother farmed at Carleton just outside Skipton, was then the national leader of the Seekers. So far as is known, there was no purpose-built Seeker meeting place in Skipton. Though no doubt they would have met in small numbers in one another's homes, the Seekers would also have required a larger space for their regional and other gatherings. The meeting house in Airton would have provided just such a place: remote, unobtrusive and easily accessible from a variety of directions. We cannot prove that the Airton Meeting House was purpose-built in the first or second decade of the seventeenth century as a Seekers' meeting place, but circumstantial evidence makes it very probable that this was the case. As such, it is a uniquely important part of our cultural heritage.

However and by whomever it was used, the Meeting House was on land owned by Major General Lambert and his family, in the centre of Airton village, close to the family dower house and almost in sight of their family seat. The Lamberts must obviously have known of and approved its use. The fact that there are no early records of violent religious controversy centred on Airton, nor subsequently of such extreme persecution of Quakers as happened elsewhere in England, implies that Lambert family members, including the Major General, were active in approving and sustaining the building's use, first by Seekers and, after 1652, by Quakers. Airton's is, so far as we can discover, the oldest extant Quaker meeting house. Before then, and even more significantly, it was most probably a purpose-built Seeker meeting place. Perhaps it was their national headquarters. In this quiet, unobtrusive building Seekers and their Quaker successors met to worship unobserved by the world at large, but very much under the eyes and under the protection of the Lambert family, who most probably caused it to be built and who owned it and approved of its use for almost a century. An implication of this is that Major General Lambert was himself a protector, patron and promoter of Seeker values and their manner of worship. His actions and his writings -- especially his efforts to promote religious toleration and his personal reluctance to be closely identified with any religious faction -- are compatible with this interpretation.

1652 - 1659

When George Fox and Richard Farnsworth set off walking from *near Bradford* in May 1652, they were not wandering at random. During Fox's travels and his imprisonment in East Yorkshire in the previous year, he had met sympathetic hearers from further west and had many opportunities to plan a route and a strategy for his forthcoming travels in the Craven and Pendle areas of Yorkshire and Lancashire. Farnsworth had much local knowledge and James Nayler, with whom Fox was then a close friend, would have had many suggestions and contacts. The two men set out with the intention of contacting potentially sympathetic audiences, congregations and individuals wherever they might be found. We know from Fox's journal that he climbed Pendle Hill, east of Clitheroe. Presumably their intended destination had not been the hilltop, but the nearby community and parish of Grindleton, whose people they hoped to enlist or *convince* to their way of thinking. Perhaps it was in frustration at the Grindletonians' refusal to accept his message or perhaps in a desire to follow the example of Old Testament prophets who communed with God on mountain tops that George Fox climbed Pendle Hill.

George Fox and James Nayler spent time together in 1651. Nayler, who had been Major General Lambert's Quartermaster during the New Model Army's campaign into Scotland, would have urged Fox to visit Lambert. Nayler would also have known which officers and former officers of the New Model Army were most likely to be receptive to Fox's message and preaching. Among these would have been leaders of the Seeker community such as Thomas Taylor and Gervase Benson.

In a heavily-edited journal that was written many years after the events it describes, Fox says that in the evening after climbing Pendle Hill, he had a vision of a great people in the north waiting to be gathered. Recent Quaker hagiography has put undue emphasis on this experience, to which no particular importance was attached at the time it occurred. Neither his travelling companion, Richard Farnsworth, nor any of Fox's contemporaries mention it in any of their many writings. The event can be given a mundane explanation. In order to get from the Bradford area to Grindleton or to Pendle Hill, Fox and Farnsworth would have had to go by way of Skipton. This was the most practical route and in any case they would have wanted to preach in the market town. While in Skipton, they must have made contact with and won at least the interest of Seeker leaders. We know that this happened because of what followed a few weeks later, when Fox went to preach at the Seekers' annual meeting at Sedbergh. In his journal he says that before preaching in the church there and to large audiences outdoors, he went first to a meeting of Seeker leaders that was being held at the home of Gervase Benson, where he was well received. Fox could only have known of this private meeting if he had been told in advance of its place and time. Had he intruded where he had not been invited, it is most unlikely that he would have been so well received or invited to preach to the assembled Seekers. Furthermore, it can be surmised that an unusually large number of Seekers were present in Sedbergh because they knew in advance that George Fox would be there and they wanted to hear what he had to say.

Margaret Fell, who is sometimes described as the Founding Mother of Quakerism, was immediately convinced of the rightness of George Fox's message when she heard him preach in the church at Sedbergh. It may well be asked how a lady of her elevated social status came to be joining farmers and common people in attending a hiring fair? The most likely answer is that, at least among Seekers, it was widely known in advance that George Fox would be preaching at their annual meeting and that she along with many others had gone to Sedbergh not to attend the fair, but to hear what this enthusiastic young man had to say.

George Fox and Richard Farnsworth may have revisited Skipton on their way north from Pendle Hill, or they could have bypassed the town by going through Gisburn and Hellifield. Perhaps they spent a few days in Airton. Farnsworth may have travelled with Fox to Airton, but we hear nothing of his having continued to accompany Fox on his further travels. He could have returned to Skipton by way of Rylstone while Fox went northwards to Bordley, four miles from Airton; both Bordley and Scale House, near Rylstone, were the homes of active early Quakers. From Bordley, a well-travelled route of about ten miles goes along Mastile's Lane to Kilnsey and then up Wharfedale to Scar House near Hubberholme, where Fox may have spent some days before continuing to Sedbergh. He visited Scar House several times in later years and some large Quaker gatherings were held there. An early Quaker burial ground at Scar House had originally been set aside for Seeker interments.

As well as winning the interest and approval of Seeker leaders in Skipton and an invitation to attend their forthcoming meetings in Sedbergh, Fox would have wanted approval or at least tacit acceptance by the Seekers' patron, Lambert. He would also have sought an opportunity to meet with and preach to local Seekers in their Meeting House in Airton. The Major General was almost certainly at home in Calton during the last week of May and first weeks of June 1652, which was a particularly difficult time in his career. While there is no written record of George Fox and Richard Farnsworth having visited Lambert and preached to Seekers in Airton in June 1652, it is most probable that they did so. In any event, there is good documentary evidence that Quaker meetings were well established at Airton by the mid 1650s.

Arrived in Sedbergh, George Fox met with the Seeker leaders and preached several times to large congregations. The result was the partial merger of two allied religious movements, which adopted a new name: Quakers. The Seekers brought to this merger a system of local and regional or national meetings, numerous supporters, a quiet dislike of public exhibitionism, and the practice of unstructured silent worship. George Fox and his friends brought a tremendous rush of youthful energy, faith, enthusiasm, sense of purpose and willingness to engage in public disputes. In its earliest years, the newly formed Seeker-Quaker community seems to have continued with much of the Seekers' organisation and leadership. Holding their regional and national meetings of leaders and their more widely attended yearly meetings in and near Skipton, they sent out epistles from Skipton, Rylstone, Bordley and Scar House. During this time, silent meetings were held at least weekly at Airton. David Hall, a prominent Skipton Quaker schoolmaster of the next generation, describes these meetings in the mid 1650s in a memorial of the life of his father, who lived in Airton and had been a tailor to Major General Lambert.

1660 - 1710

The year of the Restoration of the Monarchy, 1660, was of great importance in formation of the Quaker ethos. With the arrest of Major General Lambert in that year, Seekers lost their chief promoter and protector and the continued existence of the Seeker and Quaker religious movements may have seemed in jeopardy. In a defensive reaction, Quakers emphasised their pacifist inclinations, downplayed or denied their radical roots among Seekers and in the New Model Army, and moved their headquarters to London, thus reducing the influence of northern, Seeker, leadership. Most Quaker journals and histories, including those of George Fox, were written and edited after 1660 by authors who were acutely aware of the need to present Quakerism as a non-threatening element in society. Most stringently removed from Quaker thought and writing was any hint of association with John Lambert, of the Meeting House at Airton which his family continued to own, and of the Friends who continued to worship there. David Hall, for example, described his father not as having been tailor to the Lambert family, but as having made clothing for *one of the greatest in the land.*

Although not referred to in contemporary Quaker writings, probably because it remained too closely associated with the Lambert family and Lambert estate, Airton continued to be used as a regular Quaker meeting place. The first known Quaker burial at Airton was in 1663; there may have been earlier, unrecorded Seeker and Quaker burials. Twenty recorded burials up to 1700 suggest that during the second half of the seventeenth century the Meeting House and its grounds served a community of about 40 or 50 adults. Not everyone who attended Quaker meetings in Airton would have lived in this village. Seventeenth and early eighteenth century burials in our Meeting House yard are of people whose places of residence are listed as Airton, Bell Busk, Fleits, Gargrave, Hanlith, Kirkgillhouse, Knowlebank, Malham, Otterburn, and Winterburn, all of which are within about four miles of Airton. At the same time, there were also well-established Quaker meetings in Rylstone, Skipton and Settle. After the 1689 Act of Toleration, which abolished some of the earlier harsh penalties against Quaker and other non-conformist forms of worship, more Quaker meeting houses were built, including one in open countryside at Farfield, between Addingham and Bolton Abbey in 1689 and one in Skipton in 1693. Unlike the Airton Meeting House, these were constructed with no attempt at concealment, but are nevertheless in a very plain style, in keeping with Friends' ethos.

Fig. 11

Two active and influential Quakers in the late seventeenth century were William and Alice Ellis, who lived across the road from the Airton Meeting House. They employed apprentices and workmen in a prosperous workshop of hand-powered weaving looms. The Ellises each gave much of their time and energy to supporting Quakerism, he travelling to North America as a minister, she travelling more locally, supporting Quaker women's involvement in church affairs and welcoming visiting Friends who travelled in the ministry. Letters from William Ellis refer to Airton Meeting. In one he mentions that meetings were held midweek as well as on Sundays and was concerned that his apprentices should not sleep during meetings for worship. In another letter, William Ellis said that *some years before* they *got up* the Meeting House at Airton. In the language of the time, *got up* meant not that they built the building, but that they refurbished or furnished it. He also says that *large meetings* were held at Airton. Both of these letters were written in 1697.

Fig. 12

Fig. 13

A roughly-shaped sandstone disc, approximately 3 inches in diameter and a little less than 1/2 inch thick was found when a new grave was dug in 2015. Occasional finds of similar discs have been made in the area between Bradford and Pendle, including at Wycoller, near Colne. According to information on the finds register of the Portable Antiquities Scheme of the Department of Culture Media and Sport, these discs may have been used on a small hand-loom "as a weighted core for winding balls of yarn around them as part of a crude creel for making a warp. This would be in lieu of [wooden] bobbins ...." We can at least imagine that this object, which shows subtle traces of use-wear, was fashioned and handled by one of the Ellis employees.

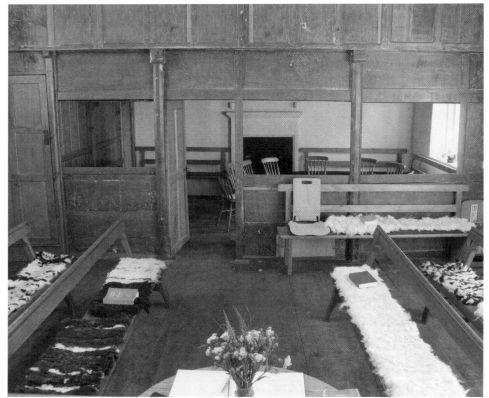

Fig. 14

Refurbishment of the Meeting House, which was extensive, was done in about 1694, a few years before William and Alice rebuilt their own house. Work at this time may have involved raising the Meeting House roof and inserting the present gallery, which would most likely have had a plain front railing. Oak wainscotting was installed on the ground-floor walls and the large room divided by inserting an internal screen with top-hinged shutters. Room-divider screens with hanging shutters, of which this is probably the earliest, best dated and most complete example in a Quaker meeting house, are a frequent feature of eighteenth century meeting houses. Skipton Meeting House's single room was divided by a wooden partition wall with similarly hinged shutters in 1761. Airton's screen and the matching oak panelling elsewhere in the room are partly dated by the shutters' nail-fastened, butterfly-shaped hinges.

Fig. 15

We may speculate that the shuttered screen was designed by Alice Ellis in order to provide women Friends with a separate room in which to conduct their own business meetings, where issues such as the education of children, placement of apprentices and care of the needy were dealt with. After meeting to worship together, men and women Friends would have separated for their business meetings. When their deliberations were completed, the shutters would be raised so that the two groups could report to one another.

Fig. 16

As part of the same work of improving the Meeting House in about 1694, a raised ministers' stand, or bench, was put across its west end, blocking a possible doorway between the meeting room and the attached cottage or stable. At the same time, a small window was broached in the north wall of the Meeting House to provide light to the raised bench; new windows may also have been inserted or windows modified in the south wall. Later, when the widowed Alice had the cottage rebuilt and put a canopy and inscribed stone with her and her husband's initials over the Meeting House doorway, these windows were enlarged, probably by lowering their sills. Some work may also have been done in about 1694 in the, then single-storey, cottage. After these improvements, furnishings in the Meeting House would have looked similar to those which can be seen at Farfield, where a Quaker meeting house was purpose-built in 1689. By 1710, the one or two rooms at the west end of the Airton Meeting House were no longer used as a cottage, but served to stable the horses of Friends coming to meetings.

Fig. 17

Fig. 18

In 1700, the Ellises paid £31 to purchase from the Lambert estate the field that included the Quaker burial ground and *that one house, barn, stable or other building* situated on this land. Even after several generations of use as a meeting house, it seems there remained a reluctance to identify the building as such. They endowed these together with their own home and and several parcels of fields and grazing rights in Airton to Quaker trustees. The Ellises' purchase of the land and building was in anticipation of the breaking up of the Lambert estate, which was completed in 1701. By then the Airton Meeting House had served as a place of worship for about three-quarters of a century or perhaps for longer, used first by Seekers then by Quakers, during which time it had remained in Lambert family ownership and under Lambert protection.

In 1710, recently widowed Alice Ellis had much work done to the property, giving it the layout and character which we now enjoy. It is recorded that she replaced a small stable adjacent to the Meeting House with a warden's cottage. In fact, she retained the original footprint and fireplace of the old ground-floor living-room and parlour or pantry, to which she added an upper floor, making a standard two-up two-down early eighteenth century cottage. The original south-facing cottage door and window were blocked by a stairway and a new door and windows were inserted in the cottage's north wall, facing the street. An internal door at the foot of the cottage staircase retains a somewhat elaborate early eighteenth century hinge. At the same time, a new stable was built facing west onto the village green and onto a no-longer-extant lane, at right angles to the line of the Meeting House and cottage, but not attached to it. This was to accommodate the horses of Friends coming to meetings. Above the stables was a loft to store hay for those horses, gathered from a field bequeathed to Friends by the Ellises. A blocked gateway to that hayfield remains visible in the south wall of the Meeting House yard. In the Meeting House, she added a chimney and two fireplaces to the east gable wall, enlarged the windows in the south wall and added a canopy over the door. The Meeting House gallery may have been installed at the same time, unless it had been constructed as part of the earlier refurbishment in about 1694. Probably she raised the Meeting House roof in line with the rebuilt cottage.

Fig. 19

Fig. 20

An inscribed stone above the door reminds us of the generous part Alice and her husband played in purchasing the Meeting House and grounds from the Lambert estate and ensuring their continued use for Quaker worship. This stone is sometimes incorrectly interpreted as indicating the date of the Meeting House's construction. While some early Quaker meeting houses, including those in Skipton and in Settle, do have dated lintels, they do not include personal initials. We may wonder if perhaps, at a time when Quakers did not erect gravestones, Alice Ellis had this memorial placed over the door as a way of commemorating her and her husband's significant role in helping Quakerism to make the transition from its turbulent beginnings to a more settled eighteenth century identity.

Fig. 21

Later alterations

Nineteenth and early twentieth century alterations to the buildings are not all well recorded or dated. The need for new stables in 1710 implies that large meetings continued into that century, with worshippers coming from further than the immediate neighbourhood. Probably late in the eighteenth century, the Meeting House was re-floored and refurbished, with a new facing bench and good-quality pine panels in the larger meeting room replacing oak wainscotting that was transferred to the front of the gallery above the hanging shutters. The addition of a porch to the cottage and the reconfiguration of its somewhat awkward looking ground floor windows facing the road are probably attributable to the early or mid nineteenth century. Until 2016, The Nook retained an uninsulated, mid nineteenth century back-pointed roof.

Probably in the third or fourth quarter of the eighteenth century, the ground floor of the stable which Alice Ellis had built in 1710 was extended and joined to the cottage by the addition of a porch or cart shed with a wide doorway in its west wall and a somewhat narrower doorway in its east wall. In about 1840, the stable and hayloft was re-roofed and given a massive new truss. At the same time or perhaps subsequently, the hay loft over the stable was extended over the cart shed to abut The Nook. In the late nineteenth century this building became known as The Barn and must then have been used as such. During restoration work in 2010, a tooth and two bones of a small breed of pig and a single cow's bone were found in soil excavated from The Barn floor.

As time passed, Quaker numbers and attendances at meetings for worship declined and the buildings survived more by neglect than by good care. In the the first decades of the twentieth century, the upper floor of The Barn was used by itinerant peddlers as a place to display their wares. The building was then referred to as *The Klondike* because no one knew in advance what treasures might be offered for sale. At the end of the nineteenth century, by which time meetings for worship were attended by just a few elderly Friends, an adult school was started. Eventually, this became The Yorkshire Adult Summer Schools, which continued at least into the mid 1930s. It may have been in conjunction with the adult schools that a large window was put into the north wall of the Meeting House and a tiled grate inserted in the fireplace in the small meeting room.

Fig. 22

For about two years during the Second World War, the Meeting House provided accommodation for two evacuee families from Liverpool, one mother and two children sleeping in the gallery, another mother and two children accommodated in the small meeting room, while Quaker meetings for worship continued to be held in the larger room. Both families used the ground floor of The Barn as their kitchen and sitting room; its first floor was by then dangerously rotten and inaccessible. Some refurbishment was done in the Meeting House to accommodate the two families. After the war, The Barn was re-roofed and a new first floor installed, supported by massive oak beams which may previously have been part of its roof structure. Unfortunately, when the building was extensively refurbished in 2011 these timbers could not be saved as they were crumbling with rot, leaving the floor perilously unsupported.

During much of the second half of the twentieth century, The Barn was used as a hostel by young Quakers and other youth groups. Although there was no longer a regular Quaker meeting for worship at Airton, well-attended meetings were held two or three times a year. During this time the cottage continued to be occupied, but inadequate attention was devoted to maintaining the buildings. By 2000, when Friends appointed a new committee to manage the property, the Meeting House was partly unroofed, its gallery dangerously unsupported, and there was much damp penetration through its cracked walls.

Fig. 23

Although The Barn was still being used for occasional hostel accommodation, it had to be temporarily closed on account of multiple health, safety and fire risks. In 2000, a few Friends who recognised the simple beauty of the Airton Meeting House, but did not then know of its historic significance, decided to reinstate regular meetings for worship at Airton and to raise sufficient funds to repair and restore the property, a decision in which they were not always well supported by others of more cautious disposition. Some Friends would have preferred that all or part of the property be sold so that the money raised could be applied to what they considered to be more worthy purposes. However, as the result of a strenuous fund-raising campaign, the Meeting House was re-roofed in 2005 and restored in 2008. The Barn, which was completely rebuilt internally, was reopened in 2011. At the same time, the garden walls were rebuilt, the shed repaired, and the cottage was largely restored to its eighteenth century configuration.

Fig. 24

Fig. 25

Quaker meetings for worship are held in our Meeting House on the second and fourth Sundays of each month at 3 o'clock in the afternoon. We are always glad to welcome visitors. Please join us if you would like to. For more information about the Airton Meeting House and about The Religious Society of Friends, please contact our Resident Friend. Contact details for Airton Friends Meeting can be found through the websites of Quakers in Yorkshire and of Britain Yearly Meeting of the Religious Society of Friends.

Fig. 26

Vernacular Buildings Survey

Site and setting

This survey provides an interpretation of the buildings based on an understanding of their fabric. Documentary records have not been greatly used. The building complex is in Airton civil parish and in Kirkby Malham ecclesiastical parish. It lies on the edge of the village green, on a road that descends steeply to reach the river bridge. The crossing is close to a nineteenth century textile mill built on the site of a medieval corn mill belonging to Bolton Priory. The present bridge is largely of early nineteenth century construction, with one large arch and a smaller flood arch. It is likely the bridge has been replaced many times. The hollow-ways on each river bank and the multiple routes radiating from Airton indicate the antiquity of the busy roads, which would have connected the many monastic and other holdings in this once-prosperous farming area of Craven.

Airton Meeting House occupies a prominent position in the village centre, unlike some other Quaker meeting houses that were built from old barns in former arable fields, as at Rylstone. The Quaker meeting houses in Settle and Skipton, however, were built in roads just off busy market squares. The Airton building complex now forms an L-shape enclosing the north-western corner of a rectangular yard and burial ground. It consists of the Meeting House, The Nook cottage and a three-bay barn, now converted to other uses. The Meeting House replaced an earlier building, almost certainly a cruck-framed barn. Opposite the Meeting House is a seventeenth century yeoman's farmhouse with a prominent datestone "WAE 1696" (William and Alice Ellis). William Ellis held some status in the area. Whitaker's *History of Craven* notes (p. 252) that in 1709 the widowed Alice Ellis gave 29 acres of land and moorland grazing rights to a trust for the Quakers to farm. A stone over the Meeting House doorway is inscribed WAE 1700.

The three buildings of the Airton group are all rectangular; they are separated by straight butt joints that indicate the sequence of their construction (figure 27). The Meeting House is a four-bay building that replaced a former cruck structure. In plan, it is very similar to the former meeting house at Rylstone that is now a cottage. Their fireplaces (dated 1730 at Rylstone, 1710 at Airton) are very similar in style. The Nook cottage has an "end stack/ direct entry" plan. Ground configuration in the yard at Airton reflects the underlying limestone bedrock and also indicates an earlier field wall. The south wall of the Meeting House yard retains the stone gateposts of a former entry to the field beyond. This field had an irregular outline on the 1850 Ordinance Survey map, but by 1898 the field walls had been straightened to a rectangular plan.

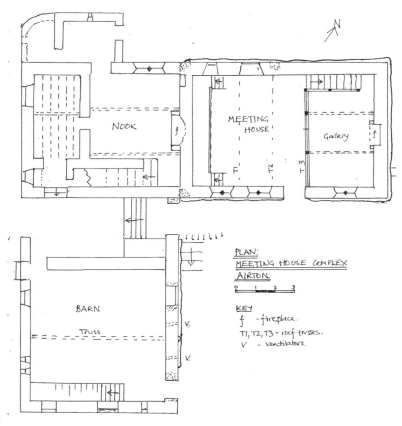

Fig. 27

The door into the Meeting House is on the south side of the building; it is reached by way of a stone gateway alongside the east gable end. It faces away from the bustle of the green and the road to the river crossing. The shape of the building complex on the 1850 map shows the Meeting House together with The Nook cottage and its porch, and then the barn at right angles. There was also in the mid nineteenth century a small building which is no longer present attached on the south gable end of The Barn.

Materials

The Meeting House walling is mainly of limestone cobbles with foundation plinths of field-clearance boulders. By contrast, sandstone boulders and cobbles are more prominent in The Nook and in The Barn, indicating different building phases. Dark limestone quoins, roughly dressed, pre-date the peck-dressed sandstone quoins of The Nook porch and The Barn. Dark limestone blocks also feature in the nineteenth century raised walls of The Barn. Dressed window surrounds of seventeenth and eighteenth century dates are of local gritstone and sandstone. Nineteenth century stone surrounds for some windows were cut by frame-saw and then tooled. Twentieth century surrounds retain traces of cutting with a frame-saw, but without hand tooling. Sandstone flags are and were used for roofing.

Interior timber in the Meeting House includes a screen of oak panels with bevelled edges. These are probably made of timber imported from the Baltic area. Comparative dates may be provided by the interior fittings at Hemplands house in Conistone, Wharfedale, (built in the 1680s); they included imported "fir deals and Norway oak" although timber for that roof was from Barden Forest. The Meeting House roof trusses are oak. They include re-used, roughly-trimmed waney oak from an earlier cruck structure of pre-1600 date. Wide softwood planks for the back of the Meeting House elders' bench were also imported.

South elevation: the Meeting House frontage and the upper gable of The Barn

The south facade (figure 28) includes the frontage of the Meeting House, which has a "basket-arch" shape of door lintel inscribed WAE 1700 (William and Alice Ellis). This stone is partly hidden by an eighteenth century door canopy or hood which has two projecting flaggy sandstone supports with broad tooling and classical ogee mouldings; The Nook porch also has ogee kneeler stones, but those are of coarser sandstone.

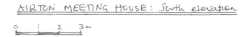

BARN   MEETING HOUSE

Fig. 28

The boulder foundation stones, which make a sort of rough plinth around the Meeting House, are from an older structure. They are cut by the Meeting House doorway. The doorway is of good dressed sandstone with "long and short" quoins. The quoins are not symmetrical. That on the left bottom forms a facing to the rough plinth; the top jamb is very narrow to fit the space below the lintel.

There is evidence that the Meeting House once had lower walls and limestone quoins and that it has been heightened in several phases. The stone walling has typical "slobbered pointing" disguising the rubble stonework which is mostly of limestone cobbles and some sandstone. On the south face, there is a line of rather large sandstones running up to a wavy joint-line with The Nook. It was fairly common for quoins to be removed at wall corners and reused for building extensions, and it is likely that this happened here. Quoins may have been removed from the south-west corner of the Meeting House and re-used in several places, which would account for the mixed quoins on the cottage. Evidence of an earlier roof-line is also seen at this joint. Above the heightened walling, at the gutter level, the foot of a re-positioned roof truss timber can be seen projecting through the wall. The ground-floor windows of the Meeting House are shallow and have typical tall, slim, mullions with lights that are wider and less deep than are usually found in seventeenth century windows. They have been enlarged by extending the mullions and side jambs to make them taller. The windows overlook the external stone bench and cut-away hillside of the Meeting House grounds. The Meeting House gallery, on the first floor, has an un-altered two-light window set in a wall that was heightened when the roof was raised.

Both chimney stacks date to approximately 1700. These also have ogee mouldings. When viewed from the south, the right-hand chimney has two pots with flues for the two Meeting House fireplaces. The left chimney is bigger; it houses two pots and flues for The Nook. This chimney sits on top of the joint wall between the Meeting House and The Nook. Owing to slight differences in roof alignments and to the The Nook and the Meeting House having been re-roofed at different times, the line of the slates on the roof between the two buildings is well-defined. The loft space inside the Meeting House roof is very soot-blackened on this joint wall.

The sandstone cobble walling of The Nook contrasts with that of the Meeting House, which is largely of limestone. The rough foundation plinth of the earliest building continues along the south wall into The Barn. It probably wrapped around the entire Meeting House area as the foundations of a three- or four-bay cruck barn. The cottage appears to have been attached to the Meeting House by using cobbles mostly of sandstone and re-using older quoin stones pulled out of the corners of the Meeting House's west gable.

The south gable end of The Barn (figure 28) shows raised eaves on the gable sides with heightened walling using dark grey limestone for walling and for small limestone quoins. These raised lines are seen also on The Barn's west and east faces. A former low opening in the centre of The Barn's south gable wall is now partly buried in the hillside; this may have been a mucking-out hole or a shippon door. One of the upper windows is modern (2011); the other is older and has a chamfered stone used for a lintel.

North elevation of the Meeting House and The Nook

On its north face, the Meeting House wall has a foundation plinth of field-clearance boulders, about 55cm high, with some large limestone quoins (figure 29). A wavy vertical walling joint separates the Meeting House on the left from The Nook on the right. The quoin stones which would have marked the end of the Meeting House were removed when the cottage was added; they were reused for the newer building end, which has mixed quoins. There are differences between the two phases left and right of this vertical joint. To the left, above the boulder plinth, are what appear to be several phases of walling. The lower portion of this wall is of well-coursed rubble with limestone quoins. Above this level and up to the top of the nineteenth century window, is walling of uncoursed rubble from further heightening that includes both the nineteenth century window and a small "reading window" dated to approximately 1700. Similar walling is also seen on the south side of the building. Quoins in the lower portion of the north face of the Meeting House include a prominent sandstone block. The eaves of the Meeting House seem to have been heightened several times, including when The Nook was added.

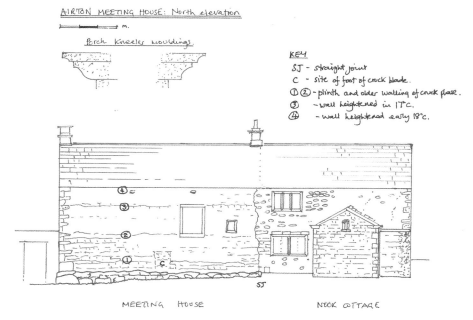

Fig. 29

The walling of The Nook, which is predominantly of orange sandstone rather than grey limestone, seems to be of mixed builds with its lower mullioned, eighteenth century, window being inserted into the wall. The large central mullion may be a re-used king mullion. The porch covers an earlier doorway with eighteenth century narrow chamfers and plinth blocks. The porch appears rather seventeenth or eighteenth century in style, with moulded coping stones, classical ogee-moulded kneelers and arched light; however, the outer doorway has a nineteenth century lintel that was constructed in a seventeenth century style. Later, probably also in the nineteenth century, a coal shed was added with access from the porch. The chimney for the cottage sits on the former gable wall of the Meeting House and is of ashlar. It looks to be about 1700 in date. A large nineteenth century projecting chimney breast in the cottage was substantially rebuilt in about 1970. Both The Nook and the Meeting House chimneys have flues for two fireplaces.

East elevation: Meeting House gable and barn

Viewed from the east (figure 30), the Meeting House's wall-plinth of clearance boulders is well seen. Its presence indicates an earlier building, probably of sixteenth century or possibly earlier construction. The quoins of the roadside elevation (north-east corner) are clearly seen, with a suggestion of a change of walling material going diagonally up the wall. The chimney flues were cut into this wall.

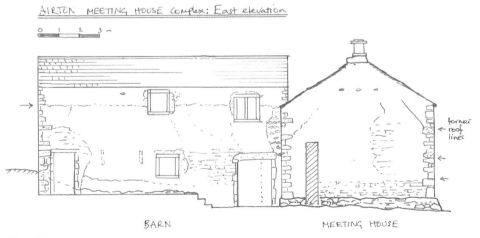

Fig. 30

The Barn once had the same eaves height as the Meeting House and The Nook. In the mid nineteenth century it was heightened and re-roofed. Most of The Barn's doors and windows date from the modern conversion and only part of the lower doorway, closest to the Meeting House, has chamfered jambs. Old photographs show this was formerly a narrow doorway. The Barn now butts against the earlier wall of The Nook, showing that it was constructed or extended after the cottage was established. The corner between The Barn and Meeting House is very disturbed by repairs and by heightening of the buildings, as seen in figures 26 and 28.

West elevation: The Nook gable and The Barn frontage

Two of the windows in the west face of The Nook (figure 31) are nineteenth century. Walling is mostly sandstone, as already noted. The lower window, lighting the under-stair pantry, has reused jambs made from window mullions. The porch and coal store project at the front. A prominent, quoined, straight joint of dark limestone separates The Nook from The Barn.

AIRTON MEETING HOUSE: West elevation

NOOK COTTAGE   BARN

Fig. 31

The Barn roof has been raised above the cottage, but was once the same height. Windows in The Barn are mostly modern. On the right, a barn forking hole with quoined sides crosses the raised walling. The central door opening is original and suggests a bank-barn plan with a hay mew on the first floor and stables below. This is a Cumbrian style. There is evidence of a former cart track across the green in front of The Barn, but this access now disappears under a modern driveway. The track would have served the low (north) end bay of The Barn, which has a cart entry with a large stone lintel. This lintel is lengthened by the use of an internal ogee corbel.

Interior detail: the Meeting House

The interior space in the Meeting House is divided into two parts by an oak screen with a gallery above (figure 27). The main meeting room is thus high-ceilinged, single storey. The east end of the building has two storeys, and rooms with fireplaces above and below. The large meeting room has a plain white plastered ceiling but this has been colour lime-washed in the past. (When the Meeting House was restored in 2008, traces of an original dark ochre-yellow lime-wash were found on the walls downstairs and brick-red lime-wash upstairs.) The ceiling of the large meeting room underdraws three roof trusses hidden above. This room's west end has a raised ministers' bench of softwood, accessed by stairs at either end that have eighteenth century Georgian ramped panelling. Floor boards are mostly wide (pre-1850) and look re-used, but the dark staining makes tree species difficult to determine. Narrow boards used in places are of subsequent date. The timber generally suggests making do or recycling of older materials.

At the east end, a gallery is supported on posts which incorporate the ceiling beams of the lower room, the balcony floor joists and the stair up to the balcony. During the 2008 restoration, it was found that the posts were intended to rest on stone supports beneath the wood floor; these were rebuilt. The gallery floor beams are heavily varnished. They have seventeenth century style lamb's-tongue chamfer stops which are barely visible as the screen and posts hide them. Being entirely within the space of the easternmost roof timbers, the gallery has a ceiling raised above that of the main meeting room. The oak screen which divides the Meeting House appears to date from around 1700, but may contain timber of different ages possibly salvaged or recycled from elsewhere. It has hinged shutters to enable communication between the two ground floor rooms. A four-panel door into the smaller meeting room under the gallery appears fragile in the way it is held together. Butterfly hinges on the top-hung shutters of the oak screen are an old style although still used in 1700. Some of the oak panels have bevelled edges suggesting they were once part of seventeenth century vertical plank and muntin panelling. A lack of knots and evidence of rather straight saw marks suggest these are not of local timber, but are seventeenth century imports from Norwegian or Baltic ports.

Fig. 32

Ironwork, too, seems attributable to a mixture of dates, but all could date to approximately1700. The six- panel door to the stair has a blacksmith-made latch. Butterfly hinges, like those on the screen shutters, are usually sixteenth and seventeenth century, but their use continued into the eighteenth century. There are are also eighteenth century L-H hinges on the front door. The two stone fireplaces each have a pediment over a very deep lintel. Their rather narrow jambs have wide chamfers and cavetto (hollow moulded) chamfer stops. Their date is early eighteenth century, probably near 1700.

Fig. 33

The Meeting House roof seems rather steeper than normal for the area. Three oak roof trusses (figure 34) can be seen in the loft space. The general form of the trusses displays a morticed apex with a square-set ridge piece. There are struts between the tie beam and the principal rafters. The original straight struts seem to have been reinforced by the addition of very curved struts. These have been seen in other seventeenth century buildings in Craven. Many of the rafters have been replaced, but the purlins, tie beams and principal rafters are made from massive oak beams with clear signs of reuse. The half-lap joinery is typical of the carpentry techniques used on local cruck structures from medieval times to early in the seventeenth century. Most date from before 1600. Those of monastic age are usually of good-quality oak supplied by the monastery. After the Dissolution, ashwood crucks were used in new barns built in the hay meadows, as in a barn at Kilnsey. One of these Meeting House trusses shows well the inward curving former cruck blades reused as principal rafters. Trenches on the outer curve of the cruck blade formerly supported purlins, whilst diagonal cuts and pegs held the horizontal tie beams and collars. Truss 3 (just inside the access hatch) exhibits a clear half-lap joint with a peg-hole probably for a wind brace. Carpenters' red chalk marking-out lines also remain. The massive purlins and tie beams were cut down from larger cruck timbers to fit this roof. Pegging seems minimal; in Wharfedale, this was common around 1700. Many of the rafters are full of nails as if they had originally held lathe and plaster. Perhaps they derive from a shippon which may have stood at the west end of the old cruck barn. A feature of the roof is extensive soot-blackening especially on The Nook chimney wall.

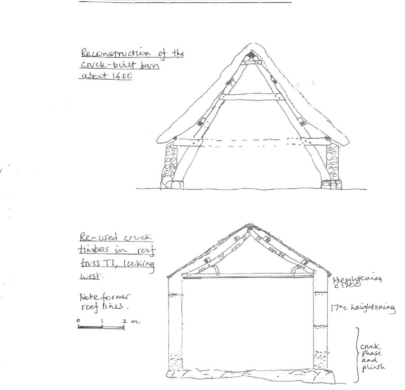

AIRTON MEETING HOUSE: ROOF TIMBERS

Reconstruction of the cruck-built barn about 1600

Re-used cruck timbers in roof truss T1, looking west.

Note former roof lines.

0   1   2 m.

Heightening c1700

17thc heightening

cruck phase and plinth

Fig. 34

The Nook

The two-bay cottage is wide, at 9 by 7 metres; its plan type is "end stack with direct entry". This is quite a common plan and also one of the simplest, with the main entry into the larger housebody room. This was the living and cooking room, the fireplace being on the gable between The Nook and the Meeting House. A second, smaller room, possibly a parlour, is now a kitchen. Beyond this was the dairy, which is partly under the stair, and is lit by a small splayed window. (During the time of the Window Tax, dairies were exempt.) A stepped doorway from the dairy into The Barn is modern.This was never a longhouse plan with house and barn joined; there is no passage cutting through the boulder plinth between The Nook and the Meeting House, and the cottage is only two cells long.

The housebody or living room is rectangular and contains the stair up. The stair has been boarded-in with tongue-and-groove planks and also 26-centimetre-wide softwood planks. The present fireplace is of gritstone with a large lintel and plain stone jambs and is probably of early nineteenth century date. It was partly rebuilt in the second half of the twentieth century. The back of the fireplace, however, is older; it has been hollowed out of the wall, making a stone-lined hood. In the wall above can be seen a large timber beam. This may be a bressumer beam which once held a timber and plaster firehood, but more probably was contrived to fit a flue against an existing stone wall. There are two spine beams across the house room, both of which finish with typically seventeenth century decorative lamb's-tongue chamfer stops. Beams in the gallery of the Meeting House share this feature, suggesting they are both of similar late seventeenth century date. A narrow recess in the window corner by the fireplace may have been a cupboard. (However, a local builder who uncovered this alcove when the cottage was restored in 2010 identified it as a former doorway into the Meeting House.)

A doorway leads from the housebody into an adjacent narrow room. Usually a room in this position is a parlour, but here there is no fireplace. The room is now lit by modern windows looking across the green. There is a good ceiling with a beam across the room and closely set joists with chamfer stops like those in the Meeting House. The timbers may be re-used; they have had some repairs where they were split and woodworm damaged. The older timbers retain some inscribed markings made with a carpenter's compass into circles and incomplete "petals". These may have been incised by a mid-twentieth century resident of The Nook who had antiquarian interests and who also carved a minute "Celtic" head on a stone corbel in The Barn. If they are pre-modern, they were possibly apotropaic (intended to avert ill luck). The six-petal flower within compass circles is an ancient symbol, often seen in barns and houses. It can be seen carved into stone doorhead designs (as at Church House in Grassington Main Street), into the seventeenth century plaster walls of a carpenter's workshop in Langcliffe, into timbers such as on the Great Barn at Bolton Priory (dendro dated 1517), and onto shippon posts in barns.

The porch kneelers, coping stones and round-headed gable light are stylistically eighteenth century. One kneeler has an ogee and one a cavetto moulding, which suggests they are re-used stones. The porch doorway is quite roughly finished inside with no internal chamfer. Although the doorhead is in a seventeenth century style, it has nineteenth century tooling that differs from that on the jamb stones. An earlier, eighteenth century doorway gave direct entry into the housebody before the porch was added. This is now an inner doorway; it has a narrow chamfer to good stonework. Also in the porch is a narrow door to an added nineteenth century coal house.

The upstairs of The Nook was not examined, but a photograph of part of the underside of the roof shows what appear to be a row of thick paired rafters fastened onto a narrow ridge timber. Paired rafters are usually medieval, but these sawn timbers look to be of mid or late nineteenth century date.

The Barn

This is a three-bay barn built down a slope. It has a heightened roof-line. Its plan seems unusual and is not a typical barn with shippon, hay storage and threshing floor. The bay nearest The Nook is separated from the other two bays by a nineteenth century stone wall replacing the usual roof truss. It looks as if there had been a ground-floor cart shed at this end and a doorway into the Meeting House yard. The jambs of an original doorway, now widened, remain accessing the paved area in front of the Meeting House; this entrance was re-opened when The Barn was refurbished in 2011. An old photograph shows possible ventilator slits on the two first-floor southern bays, which indicate hay storage. As viewed from outside, the upper right window in the west wall may have been a forking hole; this crosses the raised roof line. One would expect a forking hole in the gable but this was not seen. A ground-floor central window in the south, gable wall may have been an earlier doorway.

Fig. 35

The Barn has now been converted from agricultural use. Inside, modern (2010) stairs lead up into a community space created from the two southernmost bays. This large room has a single roof truss that rests on a heightened roofline, as seen from outside. It is a kingpost structure with struts to the kingpost and principal rafters; it is of imported, machine-sawn timber. The kingpost and principal rafters are bolted to the tie beam. There are traces of carpenter's pencil marking-out lines for the bolts. The purlins are all machine-sawn and cut to lap over the back of the principal rafters. The truss is likely to be of mid- to late-nineteenth century date, perhaps contemporary with the heightened roof. The timber has been stained but looks like imported hardwood.

Dating and interpretation

The wall foundations or plinth of limestone boulders, the lower part of the Meeting House walling with limestone quoins, and the reused cruck trusses are likely to be from the earliest building, which was probably a sixteenth century or perhaps older cruck-framed barn on the edge of the village green. The plinth extends along the south side of The Nook, but it is unclear if it is also present on the west side, now covered by the cottage. It is also unclear if the original structure was a longer building with a house attached, but this seems unlikely. This first building does not seem to have been part of a planned village layout. Houses in Cracoe, for example, are still very long buildings with a house, an attached barn and evidence of cross-passage entrances. There is documentary evidence in the sixteenth century Clifford estate surveys that such long-houses were part of a planned layout with long crofts behind each farm. The precursor of the Airton Meeting House may have originated as a barn or "field house" encroachment on the communal green near the road and river crossing. It has no evidence of a cross passage nor of associated long crofts of regular shape. This first building was rebuilt to form the Meeting House, most probably in the early seventeenth century.

Probably the old cruck timbers were saved for re-use in the usual manner and the original barn's walls were heightened to the present roof line. Using the old timbers, a carpenter made up three new roof trusses with typical morticed apex, tie beam, and principal rafters to hold the purlins. The raking struts seem to have been reinforced with very curved ones added later. There was new timber, too. Three trusses with carpenter's red chalk setting-out lines are visible in the Meeting House roof space. One reused cruck clearly shows half-lap joints for a collar, a tie beam and two sets of purlins. Some of the old cruck purlins were reused as purlins in the present roof. The old cruck frame seems to have been of oak and was possibly late medieval in date. Monastic timber was nearly always oak, whereas later a mix of oak or ash was used locally. However, the building's location on the green suggests a post-monastic date. Only dendrochronology can give an exact date of felling the tree. Timber was used green so would have been fabricated into trusses very soon after felling (see figure 34 reconstructing the cruck timber frame).

Some of the Meeting House limestone walling quoins are *in situ* and relate to an earlier, lower roof line. Some were re-positioned and were mixed with sandstone quoins during subsequent alterations and additions. In the later seventeenth century, sandstone was usual for dressed stone work, as seen here. The "basket arch" doorway is also typical of the late seventeenth and early eighteenth century; significantly, it has been cut through the earlier boulder plinth. The chimney stack is made of ashlar blocks with mouldings.

In the Meeting House, the two floor beams of the gallery have late seventeenth century lamb's-tongue stops; these are somewhat hidden by the screen panels. The same kind of stops are also seen in the two beams in the housebody of The Nook. The plain mullioned windows of the ground floor are not very deeply splayed. They and the small window that lights the gallery are typical of the late seventeenth or early eighteenth century. Ironwork latches, butterfly hinges, and L-H hinges are also attributed to the seventeenth and early eighteenth centuries. Panelling boards of imported timber from Norway and the Baltic are known from late seventeenth century houses in Wharfedale. The two fireplaces in the Meeting House look to be early eighteenths century; they have typical deep lintels with moulded sills above and chamfered jambs with cavetto chamfer stops. The Meeting House has many features that date to about 1700.

Fig. 36

The Nook, which was built or rebuilt in 1710, appears added to the Meeting House with wavy straight joints (see figures 26 and 27). These joints may be places where quoins were pulled out to reuse. Interior beams in The Nook parlour and upholding the gallery in the Meeting House have the same style of chamfer stops. The Barn seems to have been constructed in the eighteenth century, but not joined to The Nook until after about 1775, as shown on Thomas Jefferys' map, figure 4. Its plan is not of usual type and there is no sign of shippons under the hayloft floor. The cart entry is small, but may have had a granary over it. In about 1840, the barn was heightened and given a new bolted kingpost. Wall vents indicate the upper floor was used for hay storage.

Summary Timeline

Before 1600	A ling-thatched cruck barn stood in a field near the Airton cross-roads, close to the Lambert dower house.
By about 1620	The cruck barn was rebuilt as a stone-roofed Meeting House with an attached single-storey room or cottage; neither had windows or doors facing the street.
1651	George Fox spent much of this year in East Yorkshire, part of the time in prison.
May/June 1652	George Fox and Richard Farnsworth set off on foot to visit parts of West and North Yorkshire and Lancashire.
June 1652	Airton Meeting House and Major General Lambert were probably visited by George Fox while on his way from Pendle Hill to Sedbergh, where he preached to assembled Seekers. The year 1652 is considered seminal in the inception of Quakerism.
Mid 1650s	Regular Quaker meetings were held at Airton. Gervase Bensen preached here in 1657 or 1658. Several regional and national meetings of Quaker leaders were held in or near Skipton, Rylstone and Airton.
1660	Restoration of the Monarchy; Major General Lambert was imprisoned. A large Quaker yearly meeting was held in Skipton. Later that year, their national headquarters was moved to London.
1663	Earliest recorded Quaker burial at Airton.
About 1679	William Ellis established a hand-loom weavery in Airton.
1689	The Act of Toleration removed the most severe impediments imposed on Protestant Dissenters. Farfield Quaker Meeting House was built shortly before this Act was passed.
1693	Skipton Quaker Meeting House was built.
About 1694	William and Alice Ellis refurbished the Airton Meeting House: the oak woodwork, screen wall, ministers' bench and small reading window date to this time. Probably the Meeting House roof was raised and the gallery inserted.
1697	William Ellis wrote that occasional large meetings were held at Airton as well as twice-weekly meetings for worship.

1700	William and Alice Ellis purchased the Airton Meeting House and burial ground in anticipation of dispersal of the Lambert estate, which occurred in 1701. These were endowed to Quaker trustees.
1710	The old cottage was being used as a stable. Alice Ellis replaced this with a new stable and hayloft, rebuilt the cottage with an added upstairs and turned it around to face the road. Enlarged windows and two fireplaces were added to the Meeting House.
Late 18th century	The lower floor of The Barn was extended to abut The Nook. An external porch was added to The Nook. In the Meeting House, oak wainscoting was transferred to the front of the gallery; replacement pine wall panels, new floorboards and a new front bench were installed.
Mid 19th century	The roof of The Barn was raised and its first floor extended to abut The Nook. The Nook was re-roofed and an external porch added.
Late 19th / early 20th century	Quaker meetings at Airton were very small, but an adult school was started. An ungainly large window was put in the south wall of the Meeting House and a tiled grate inserted in the small meeting room's fireplace.
1942	Temporary alterations were made to The Barn and the Meeting House to accommodate two war-displaced families.
by 2000	Although they continued to be used by youth groups and for holiday accommodation, the buildings were in very poor repair, with the Meeting House partly unroofed.
2004	A local Quaker Meeting was reinstated at Airton
2005	The Meeting House was re-roofed
2008	The Meeting House and the garden walls were restored.
2010	The Nook was restored.
2011	The Barn was internally rebuilt.
2016	Following winter storm damage, much work was done to the buildings' roofs.

Notes to the Illustrations

The measured drawings and plans illustrating the vernacular buildings survey were made on site by Alison Armstrong. All the photographs used in this book are by Laurel Phillipson, with thanks to Hilary Fenten, Wilf Fenten and Tacye Phillipson for assistance with their presentation. The location map was prepared by David Phillipson.

1, inside front cover   Airton Meeting House viewed from the south with The Barn on the left: window alterations and the door canopy date to 1710. The threshold of the Meeting House entrance is well below the natural line of the hill slope.

2, page vi   Quaker meetings for worship are held in this Meeting House on Sunday afternoons. The benches with movable backs and pendant light fittings derive from the Airton Methodist church and schoolroom, which closed in 2004. The fixed bench and pine panelling at the front of the Meeting House are late eighteenth century replacements of seventeenth century furnishings that would have been similar to those in Farfield Meeting House, shown in figure 19.

3, page 4   The 1775 edition of Jefferys' map shows much interesting detail. Airton was then only a little larger than it had been a hundred years earlier. Hellifield, Otterburn, Airton (Air Town), Calton (Caulton Hall), and Bordley are on an ancient route from Clitheroe that joins Mastiles Lane near Kilnsey, some miles north of Grassington in Upper Wharfedale. It can be traced as an almost straight diagonal line, from the lower left to the upper right corner on this portion of the map. Probably George Fox went this way when he walked from Pendle Hill to Sedbergh in June 1652. It is the most direct and least hilly route into Wharfedale from the south-west. Interestingly, unlike Bordley and villages further north in Wharfedale which George Fox probably visited, no records have been found that mention early seventeenth century Quakers in Grassington or Threshfield, both of which he would have bypassed.

4, page 6   Although this detail from Jefferys' map is not entirely accurate as to the road layout, it is correct in showing the Meeting House and cottage conjoined and The Barn, built in 1710, as a detached structure. The Barn then faced onto a lane which no longer exists.

5, page 7   High Laithe, the restored ling-thatched stone barn at Grimwith Reservoir, is a late example of a simple cruck barn, with a two-bay barn on the right and a one-bay room on the left. The first building on the site of the Airton Meeting House would have been of similar construction and appearance, but larger and perhaps with a stout wall and chimney between its two rooms.

6, page 9   Airton Meeting House was constructed, probably early in the seventeenth century, on the rough foundation of an earlier barn. Particularly on its eastern end and along its southern face the ground was cut away, exposing part of the older foundation. At the extreme left of the photograph, it can be seen that the threshold to the Meeting House entrance was cut into the top of the foundation wall.

7, page 10 Even after a small window was inserted in about 1694, the Meeting House presented a bleak exterior to the world. The upstairs cottage windows probably date to 1710, while the lower cottage windows look like later alterations. The cottage porch is an early nineteenth century addition, and the large Meeting House window belongs to the late nineteenth or early twentieth century. Although the path and iron railings in front of the Meeting House were added in 2008 in order to provide disabled access, the steps on the left mark the original access from the road and from the Ellis's home across the road.

8, page 11   The stone bench in front of the Meeting House dates to the early seventeenth century, when the Meeting House was built. It provides definite evidence that the Meeting House was purpose-built as such, since this feature would have been of no use to cattle. Its presence also suggests that the Meeting House may formerly have hosted quite large gatherings, perhaps of more people than could be accommodated inside.

9, page 12 A narrow path, cut below the foundation level of an older building, leads around the east end of the Meeting House to what was probably originally a closed door. This gateway is part of the early seventeenth century construction.

10, page 14   Looking east from the green in the centre of Airton, the Meeting House is on the right; the home of William and Alice Ellis is on the left. Beyond are the ancient site of a water-powered corn mill and a bridge over the river Aire.

11, page 19 A one-room Quaker Meeting House was built on a back lane near the centre of Skipton in 1693. David Hall, whose father began attending Quaker meetings in Airton in about 1657 or 1658, was prominent among Skipton Quakers at this time.

12, page 20   The home of William and Alice Ellis was built (or rebuilt) a few years after they got up the Airton Meeting House. It was situated between the Lambert Dower House and the Meeting House. Their front door is almost opposite the path to the Meeting House. Alongside and behind the Ellis House were the buildings of their weaving workshop and a substantial barn.

13 and 14, pages 21&22 Although the screen shutters in the Meeting House are usually kept closed to prevent them from warping, they still serve their original function. When they are opened, the Meeting House has excellent acoustics. Someone standing by the raised minister's bench at the east end of the room can easily be heard from all parts of the Meeting House and seen from the front of the upstairs gallery as well as from both the large and the small meeting rooms.

15 and 16, page 23   A notable feature of the butterfly hinges on the hanging shutters is that they were put on with nails, not with screws. The use of wood screws was uncommon before the eighteenth century. When open, the shutters are suspended by a very simple mechanism.

17, page 24   Externally, the reading light in the north wall of the Meeting House is carefully detailed. Internally, its opening is widely splayed in order to admit as much light as possible.

18, page 25 The Meeting House door canopy is a somewhat unusual feature. There is the remaining stump of what may have been a similar canopy over the original main, west, door of The Barn. Both date to 1710.

19, page 26   Farfield Quaker Meeting House was purpose built in 1689. It is a one-room building without an internal partition. Oak panelling and the provision of a raised ministers' bench in Farfield Meeting House are similar to those in the Airton Meeting House.

20, page 27   View of The Barn and The Nook (Resident Friends' cottage) from the west: part of the cottage's west wall collapsed and was rebuilt in the mid twentieth century. The original (1710) stairs to The Barn's principal entrance led onto what was then a lane leading onto the Gargrave road, but is now part of a neighbour's driveway. When The Barn was renovated in 2011, the original stone stairs had to be replaced.

As shown on Jefferys' map (figure 4), The Barn was originally a detached structure. In its north gable end (left in this photograph), there would have been an entrance to the stables on the ground floor. In the late eighteenth century, the building was extended to abut The Nook, by the addition of a ground floor cart shed. A wide entrance then faced onto the lane and village green; a corresponding, narrower door in the east wall opened onto the courtyard in front of the Meeting House (figures 24 and 36). This doorway was reinstated in 2011. The Barn's first floor was extended and its roof raised in the mid nineteenth century.

21, page 28 Especially in the seventeenth and eighteenth centuries, Quakers were concerned not to single out or memorialise individuals. They did not erect gravestones, meeting houses did not have dedication plaques, and date-stones over meeting house entrances did not usually have inscriptions or personal initials. The engraved stone over the Airton Meeting House, which commemorates its purchase from the Lambert estate in 1700, is thus most unusual in that it has the initials of William and Alice Ellis, who endowed the Meeting House together with their own home across the road and a substantial amount of additional property to Friends.

22, page 29   Before it was internally remodelled, The Barn had a sloping cement floor, which is visible in the foreground. This floor was lowered and levelled as part of the recent renovation works.

23, page 31   Some very substantial cracks in the Meeting House walls were repaired in 2008 using traditional methods and materials.

24, page 32   An older, blocked entrance to The Barn's ground floor was re-opened in 2011.

25, page 33   Restoration work in the Meeting House included removing a thick coat of grey paint that had been applied in the 1950s to all woodwork including the benches and the seventeenth century oak panelling. Remaining traces of this paint could not be removed without damaging the wood.

26, page 34   Airton Friends are pleased to welcome many visitors. Some come to view the historic buildings, some to join us in Quaker meetings for worship, others come for a wide variety of events, meetings and concerts. In one year, 2014, we had more than 11,000 visitors.

27, page 36   Plan of the buildings.

28, 29, 30 and 31, pages 38,40,41&42   South, north, east and west elevation drawings show the buildings as they are in 2016.

32 and 33, pages 44&45   Latches and "L-H" hinges on the entrance door of the Meeting House were hand-forged in the late seventeenth or early eighteenth century.

34, page 46 An early seventeenth century truss in the Meeting House roof is constructed out of reused cruck timbers. Its gentler slope as compared with its ling-thatched predecessor would have supported a stone roof. This truss was repaired and strengthened in 2016.

35, page 49 We do not know what kind of roof The Barn had when it was first built in 1710. It was replaced in the mid nineteenth century by the present roof, supported by a massive timber truss.

36 and 37, pages 51&61   We hope you will visit our Meeting House and that you will find it to be a place of welcoming tranquillity.

38, inside back cover   Location map of places mentioned in the text. Key to the insert: B = Bordley; BB = Bell Busk; C = Calton; E = Eshton; F = Fleits (Fleets); G = Gargrave; Ha = Hanlith; He = Hellifield; KB = Knowlebank (Know/Knowle Bank); KG = Kirkgillhouse (Kirk Gill); KM = Kirkby Malham; M = Malham; O = Otterburn; R = Rylstone; SH = Scale House; W = Winterburn.

References and bibliographic sources

The chief source of information on local Quakers is the unpublished archives of Craven and Keighley Area Meeting (formerly, Settle Monthly Meeting) that are deposited in the Leeds University Brotherton Library. Relevant records and documents are also held at Friends House in London, and in the archives of the Malhamdale Local History Group, who maintain an interesting and useful website. It is much regretted that no full biography of Major General Lambert has been written. Neither is there any fully researched history of the crucial first decade of Quakerism, from 1650 to 1660. Snippets of relevant information have been gleaned from many sources. The following are a few of the most useful published works which have been consulted in writing this brief history.

Backhouse, J., 1849. *The Life and Correspondence of William and Alice Ellis of Airton.* London: Charles Gilpin, and York: John Linney.

Boulton, D., 1997. The Quaker Military Alliance. *Friends Quarterly* 31,8: 393-405.

Dawson, W. H., 1882. *History of Skipton.* London: Simpkin, Marshall & Co., and Skipton: Edmondson & Co.

Dawson, W. H., 1938, *Cromwell's Understudy: the life and times of General Jonn Lambert and the rise and fall of the Protectorate*, London, Edinburgh and Glasgow: William Hodge & Co.

Farr, D. N., 2003. *John Lambert, Parliamentary Soldier and Cromwellian Major-General. 1619-1684.* Woodbridge, Suffolk: The Boydell Press.

Farr, D. N., 2000. The shaping of John Lambert's allegiance and the outbreak of the Civil War. *Northern History* 36,2: 247-66.

Hall, D., 1758. *Some Brief Memoirs of the Life of David Hall, with an Account of the Life of his Father, John Hall.* London: Luke Hinde.

Harland, R., 1993. *The Living Stones of Skipton Quaker Meeting.* Skipton: Skipton Preparative Meeting of the Religious Society of Friends.

Hill, C., 1958., *Oliver Cromwell 1658-1958*. London: Routledge and Kegan Paul for the Historical Association.

Hurtley, T., 1786. *A concise Account of some Natural Curiosities in the Environs of Malham, in Craven, in Yorkshire*. London: Logographic Press.

Jones, R.M., 1909. *Studies in Mystical Religion*. London: Macmillan & Co.

Penny, N., (Editor) 1907. *The First Publishers of Truth*. London: Headley Brothers.

Penny, N., (Editor) 1911. *The Journal of George Fox*. Cambridge: Cambridge University Press.

Sewel, W., 1811 (5th edition). *The history of the Rise, Increase and Progress of the Christian People Called Quakers*. London: William Phillips.

Sharp, W., 1990. *A History of Airton Mill*. Skipton: published by the Author.

Thistlethwaite, W. P., 1979. *Yorkshire Quarterly Meeting of the Society of Friends, 1665-1966*. Harrogate: published by the author.

Waterfall, A., n.d. *Memoirs.* unpublished manuscript owned by the family of Roger Waterfall.

Watts, M. R., 1978 (reprint 2002). *The Dissenters*. Oxford: Oxford University Press.

Whitaker, T. D., 1973. reprint of the 3rd edition (1878). *The History and Antiquities of the Deanery of Craven in the County of York*. Manchester and Skipton: E. J. Morten and The Craven Herald.

Wright, S., 2006. Town and Country: Living as a Friend in Urban and Rural Yorkshire 1780-1860. *The Journal of the Friends Historical Society* 61, 1: 3-31.

Fig. 37

About the authors

Alison Armstrong has had a career in museums (geology and natural history) and was Natural Sciences Curator for the Bradford Museums Service. She has always had an interest in "old buildings" and is a member of the Yorkshire Vernacular Buildings Study Group and the national Vernacular Architecture Group. She has studied and published reports on many of Craven's vernacular buildings and has provided many short courses and day-schools for local enthusiasts. Examining vernacular buildings is a relatively new study and there is much to discover. Sciences such as dendochronology are now adding to the available dating methods and are pushing back the dates of our earliest local buildings into the sixteenth century.

Laurel Phillipson has an archaeologist's interest in the material evidence of peoples' lives and actions. She has published much on rather specialised aspects of African prehistory and a little on early Quaker history, including articles on Quakerism in Cambridge and a transcription of the eighteenth-century Wisbech Quakers Roll. She is a member of Airton Local Meeting of the Religious Society of Friends (Quakers), has been very involved with the restoration of the Airton Trust Property, continues to work as an archaeologist in Ethiopia, and is happily married with two children who have long since grown and flown the nest.

Chris Skidmore is a retired University lecturer with a keen interest in the history and architecture of Nonconformist places of worship. He is on the Council of the Chapels Society and serves as its honorary editor. He is preparing an edition of the seventeenth century Minute Books of Reading Monthly Meeting for the Berkshire Record Society. Other interests include Quaker scientists and physicians, the history of London Yearly Meeting and how Quakers have dealt with internal conflict through their history. Brought up attending a Congregational Chapel, he has been for 30 years an active Quaker, serving both nationally and locally. He worships regularly at both Airton and Skipton Quaker meetings.